SMALL BUSINESS INFORMATION SHARING: COMBATING FOREIGN CYBER THREATS

HEARING

BEFORE THE

COMMITTEE ON SMALL BUSINESS
UNITED STATES
HOUSE OF REPRESENTATIVES

ONE HUNDRED FIFTEENTH CONGRESS

SECOND SESSION

HEARING HELD
JANUARY 30, 2018

Small Business Committee Document Number 115–053
Available via the GPO Website: www.fdsys.gov

U.S. GOVERNMENT PUBLISHING OFFICE

28–359   WASHINGTON : 2018

CONTENTS

OPENING STATEMENTS

WITNESSES

APPENDIX

SMALL BUSINESS INFORMATION SHARING: COMBATING FOREIGN CYBER THREATS

TUESDAY, JANUARY 30, 2018

House of Representatives,
Committee on Small Business,
Washington, DC.

The Committee met, pursuant to call, at 11:00 a.m., in Room 2360, Rayburn House Office Building. Hon. Steve Chabot [chairman of the Committee] presiding.

Present: Representatives Chabot, Radewagen, Kelly, Blum, Comer, Fitzpatrick, Marshall, Norman, Velázquez, Evans, Lawson, Chu, Espaillat, and Schneider.

Chairman CHABOT. Good morning. I call this hearing to order. We want to thank everyone for being here.

Over the past few years, this Committee has focused its attention on an issue that is become increasingly important for small businesses, cybersecurity. In past hearings, we have learned that a cyber attack on a small business can have serious consequences, not only for the business itself, but for its customers and employees and business partners alike. We have heard from small business owners and cybersecurity experts and government officials, and there is no question that improving cybersecurity for America's small businesses should continue to be a top priority, especially for this Committee.

In today's global economy, small businesses are increasingly turning to foreign technology to remain competitive in the world marketplace. However, these same products and services also provide new opportunities for foreign cyber criminals to infiltrate small business information technology systems, allowing them to access sensitive and valuable information.

A recent survey found that 81 percent of small businesses are concerned about a cyber attack, but only 63 percent have the most basic cybersecurity measures in place to combat such an attack.

Cyber attacks pose a higher risk for small businesses, since most do not have the means to hire specialized employees or pay the average $32,000 in damages should they be hit with a cyber attack. And, cyber threats for small businesses are on the rise.

This Committee has also found that the federal government is stepping up its efforts to both prevent and mitigate cyber attacks by coordinating and distributing cybersecurity resources directly to small businesses. There is strong bipartisan support from both chambers of Congress and the President to increase American protection from foreign cyber attacks.

However, small businesses are still hesitant to engage with the federal government. This is often due to uncertainty surrounding legal liabilities, concerns about privacy and data protection, and a number of other factors. Still, federal information sharing is crucial to ensuring that small businesses have every resource possible to combat cyber threats and the confidence they need to engage with the federal agencies tasked with protecting them.

That is why the Ranking Member and I recently introduced H.R. 4668, the Small Business Advanced Cybersecurity Enhancements Act of 2017, to increase the defensive measures available for small businesses undergoing or concerned about a cyber attack, and to incentivize additional information sharing between the private sector and the federal government.

This bipartisan legislation seeks to safeguard small business from cyber attacks in a few simple ways. First, the bill establishes Small Business Development Centers, SBDCs, as the primary liaison for federal information sharing for small businesses. This bill also ensures that small businesses that engage with SBDCs receive the same protections and exemptions provided by the Cybersecurity Information Sharing Act, or CISA.

Further, this bill would ensure that any policies or rulemaking adopted by any federal agency as a result of federal information sharing does not unfairly burden small businesses. It would also expand liability protections for small businesses and engage with the federal government in good faith. Ultimately, this legislation removes the barriers many small business owners face when confronted with a cyber threat, encouraging them to work with the federal government, not fear it.

As I mentioned before, many cyber threats towards small businesses come at the hands of foreign bad actors, sometimes foreign governments, in an attempt to undermine the United States' national security and economy. In fact, the Department of Homeland Security recently published a public notice exposing a vulnerability in a notable security camera company. Hikvision, one of the top five largest manufacturers of security cameras worldwide, is 42 percent owned by the Chinese government, and in 2017, the Department of Homeland Security learned that many of its cameras were able to be hacked and remotely controlled. While Hikvision has worked with DHS to remedy the flaw, the problem remains that many small businesses that do not engage with the government or DHS regularly, and that is probably the majority of them, may not be even aware of the security flaw. Had the problem gone unnoticed, many small businesses would not have known that they were vulnerable to attack.

So we look forward to hearing from our witnesses here today to learn more about how the federal government is working to address these important problems, and further, what preventative measures small businesses can use to protect themselves from falling victim to cyber attacks.

And I would now like to yield to the Ranking Member, Ms. Velázquez, for her opening statement.

Ms. VELÁZQUEZ. Thank you, Mr. Chairman.

Ever since Russia used cyber attacks to influence the outcome of our 2016 elections, cybersecurity has been thrust to the forefront of national discussions. In today's world, everything from editorial integrity, to national security, to private sector trade secrets are at risk of cyber exploitation.

In recent years, cybercriminals have increasingly targeted small businesses. Forty percent of all cyber attacks are focused on companies with less than 500 employees. This may be because only 14 percent of small businesses reported having in place a plan for keeping their company cyber secure.

Among the most prolific users of cyber attacks are Chinese and Russian companies. In particular, a Chinese company has been documented to target American small businesses in order to obtain backdoor access to trade secrets and national security information.

As hackers and other bad actors, including foreign agents, continue to evolve their cyber attacks, strengthening the federal government's engagement with small firms is crucial. The agencies we will hear from today are on the forefront of that fight. The FBI, which is testifying today, has worked with the Small Business Administration to develop InfoGard, a collaborative effort to conduct regional workshops to counsel small firms on cybersecurity. The Department of Homeland Security, which is also represented in our panel, has created a new effort requiring private companies pursuing government contracts to be held to the same standards as the awarding agency to strengthen cybersecurity.

While the goal of this effort is laudable, we must ensure that small firms have the resources to meet new cybersecurity requirements. To this end, I am proud to join the Chairman on H.R. 4668, the Small Business Advanced Cybersecurity Enhancements Act of 2017. This bill will establish a central small business cybersecurity assistance unit coordinated by SBA and federal agencies, including DHS. Furthermore, the act will create a regional small business cybersecurity assistance unit within each Small Business Development Center, or SBDC. This will help to bring much needed hands-on cybersecurity training to small firms across the country.

Today's hearing is an opportunity to learn more about the government efforts, specifically DHS and the FBI, to assist small businesses in the protection of themselves and the government's national security.

So let me thank all of our witnesses for testifying today. I would like to especially acknowledge the men and women serving in all divisions of the FBI. We know that you do extraordinary work under challenging circumstances and that your agency, unfortunately, sometimes comes under political fire. Now more than ever, we need skilled, impartial professionals serving in the Bureau, and so we thank you for the work that you and your colleagues do.

With that, let me thank all witnesses for being here today. I look forward to today's hearing and I yield back the balance of my time.

Chairman CHABOT. Thank you very much. The gentlelady yields back.

Now I would like to explain very briefly relative to our timing and things, and I would also say that if Committee members have opening statements they can please submit them for the record.

And we operate under the 5-minute rule here. Basically, each of you gets 5 minutes to testify and then we get 5 minutes to ask questions back and forth, Republican, Democrat.

There is a lighting system. The green light will be on for 4 minutes. The yellow light will be on for a minute to let you know it is getting time to wrap up, and then the red light will come on, and we would hope you could stay within those parameters. We will give you a little leeway.

And I would now like to introduce our distinguished panel here; small, but very distinguished.

Our first witness today is Mr. Howard Marshall. He has served as Deputy Assistant Director of the Cyber Intelligence Outreach and Support Branch at the FBI since August 2016. In this role, Mr. Marshall works to identify and defeat cyber threats targeting the United States through strategic partnerships and intelligence coordination. Mr. Marshall began his career with the FBI in 1997 and has held a variety of positions both inside and outside of the Cyber Division. And we thank you for being here today.

And our second witness will be Mr. Richard Driggers. Mr. Driggers serves as the National Protection and Programs Directorate Deputy Assistant Secretary for the Office of Cybersecurity and Communications at the Department of Homeland Security. And if that is not the longest title we have had in this Committee ever, it is pretty close. And he is responsible for developing and implementing operational programs to strengthen the security of the nation's critical infrastructure.

Mr. Driggers joined DHS in 2003, and most recently was the Principal Deputy Director for Operations for the National Cybersecurity and Communications Integration Center. He is also a former United States Air Force combat controller. We thank you very much for your service and for being here today, both you gentlemen. We appreciate it.

And Mr. Marshall, you are recognized for 5 minutes.

STATEMENTS OF HOWARD MARSHALL, DEPUTY ASSISTANT DIRECTOR, CYBER DIVISION, FEDERAL BUREAU OF INVESTIGATION; RICHARD DIGGERS, DEPUTY ASSISTANT SECRETARY, OFFICE OF CYBERSECURITY AND COMMUNICATIONS, NATIONAL PROTECTION AND PROGRAMS DIRECTORATE, UNITED STATES DEPARTMENT OF HOMELAND SECURITY

STATEMENT OF HOWARD MARSHALL

Mr. MARSHALL. Chairman Chabot, Ranking Member Velázquez, and members of the Committee.

Chairman CHABOT. And if you would not mind just pulling the mic a little closer.

Mr. MARSHALL. Sure.

Chairman CHABOT. Make it easier for the folks out there to hear. Thank you.

Mr. MARSHALL. Thank you for the invitation to provide remarks on the FBI's role in helping small businesses defend against cyber threats. We consider engagement with the private sector to be a significant factor in our mission to identify, pursue, and defeat nefarious cybercriminals and enemies of the United States.

As the Committee is well aware, the growing number and sophistication of cyber threats poses a critical risk to U.S. businesses and the impact of a successful attack can be devastating to small businesses in particular. We continue to see an increase in the scale and scope of reporting on malicious cyber activity that can be measured by the amount of corporate data stolen or deleted, personally identifiable information compromised, or remediation costs incurred by U.S. victims.

Some of the more prevalent arising cyber threats to small businesses from both domestic and foreign cyber actors include business email compromise; ransomware; the criminal targeting of data, including customer data, financial data, or intellectual property; and the growing risk posed by vulnerabilities of IOT devices, Internet of Things.

In light of these and other cyber threats to U.S. businesses, the FBI has made private sector engagement a key component of our strategy for combatting cyber threats. Recognizing the ever-changing threat landscape, the FBI is enhancing the way it communicates with private industry. Traditionally, the Bureau has used information developed through its investigations shared by intelligence community partners or provided by other law enforcement agencies to understand the threat posed by nation states and criminal actors.

However, we are now also looking to integrate private industry information into our intelligence cycle to enhance our ability to identify, prioritize, and respond to both emerging and ongoing threats. Private industry has unique insight into their own networks and may have information as to why their company or their sector may be an attractive target for malicious cyber activity. Companies may also be able to share intelligence on the types of attempted attacks they experience. We believe it is important the FBI integrate this type of data into its own intelligence cycle. This type of information sharing enables us to provide more specific, actionable, and timely information to our industry partners so they can protect their systems in a proactive manner.

The FBI disseminates information regarding specific threats to the private sector through various reporting mechanisms. Public service announcements published by the Internet Crime Complaint Center provide timely and practical information to U.S. businesses and individuals on the latest threats of scams. Private industry notifications, PINs, offer contextual information about ongoing or emerging cyber threats and FBI liaison alert system reports provide technical indicators gleaned through investigations or intelligence. These communication methods facilitate the sharing of information with a broad audience or specific sector and are intended to provide recipients with actionable intelligence to aid in victim notifications, threat neutralization, and other investigative efforts.

The FBI also believes it is critical to maintain strong relationships with our private sector partners to allow for successful responses to cyber attacks. One example of an effective public-private relationship is the National Cyber Forensic and Training Alliance, a nonprofit 501(c)(3) corporation focused on identifying, mitigating, and neutralizing cybercrime threats globally. Working hand-in-hand with private industry, law enforcement, and academia, the NCFTA's mission is to provide a neutral, trusted environment that enable two-way information sharing, collaboration, and training.

The NCFTA works directly with 136 member organizations from the banking, retail, critical infrastructure, healthcare, and government sectors. Their analysts have real-time access to FBI agents, analysts, and the actionable intelligence they collect. The FBI Cyber Division regularly coordinates initiatives for engagement with private sector partners to prevent threats and ultimately close intel gaps. In recent years, we have launched public awareness campaigns or open houses to educate businesses on serious cyber threats.

In 2016, the FBI collaborated with DHS, U.S. Secret Service, Department of Health and Human Services, and the National Council on Information Sharing and Analysis Centers to host conferences and workshops at FBI and Secret Service field offices across the country to educate businesses on the ransomware threat. The FBI and Secret Service jointly hosted these workshops in 14 key cities, targeting small, medium, and large organizations. Over 5,700 individuals were briefed during this campaign. Similarly, in 2017, the FBI collaborated with DHS, Secret Service, and NCISACs to host workshops across the country on business email compromise.

The Cyber Division engages directly with businesses in other ways as well. We host or participate in briefings, conferences, workshops, and other meetings providing strategic level information to key executives throughout industry. These briefings include both classified and unclassified discussions regarding cyber threats. Over the past 5 years, the FBI Cyber Division has completed nearly 2,800 such engagements, not counting the many informal contacts and interactions we have with businesses in our field offices on a regular basis.

When a small business has been victimized by a cybercrime and reaches out to the FBI for assistance, we coordinate with the individual business to determine the best course of action to address the incident. The FBI's approach in working with potential actual victims of cyber intrusions or attacks is to first and foremost, and to the best of our ability, use our processes to protect the victim from being revictimized. We at the FBI appreciate the Committee's efforts in making cyber threats to small businesses a focus and to committing to improving how we can work together to better defend U.S. businesses from cyber adversaries.

We thank you for the opportunity to speak about our cyber outreach efforts. We look forward to discussing these issues in greater detail and answering any questions you may have.

Chairman CHABOT. Thank you very much.

Mr. Driggers, you are recognized for 5 minutes.

STATEMENT OF RICHARD DRIGGERS

Mr. DRIGGERS. Chairman Chabot, Ranking Member Velázquez, and members of the Committee, thank you for the opportunity to discuss the ongoing efforts to enhance the cybersecurity of America's small businesses.

The Department of Homeland Security serves a critical role in safeguarding and securing cyberspace, which is a core Homeland Security mission. At DHS, we assist with protecting civilian federal government networks, share information related to cybersecurity risks in an incident, and provide technical assistance to federal agencies, as well as State and local governments, international partners, and the private sector. The Department of Homeland Security, the federal Bureau of Investigation, the Small Business Administration, and other interagency partners play a crucial role in helping small businesses identify and mitigate cybersecurity risks.

Cyber threats remain one of the most significant strategic risks for the United States, threatening the national security, economic prosperity, and public health and safety. Global cyber events or incidents such as the WannaCry ransomware incident last May and the NotPetya malware incident in June are examples of malicious actors leveraging cyberspace to create disruptive effects and cause economic loss. We have also seen advanced persistent threat actors target small businesses to leverage their infrastructure and their relationships with larger businesses to gain access to networks of major and high-value assets that operate components of the Nation's critical infrastructure. DHS has confidence that these threat actors are actively pursuing their ultimate long-term campaign goals, and DHS and the FBI remain ever-vigilant and active with incident response and have published multiple joint technical alerts to enable network defenders to identify and take action to reduce exposure to malicious activity.

These incidents remind us that small businesses play a key role in ensuring the security, reliability, and resilience of the Nation's critical infrastructure and that small businesses can be easy targets across a complex attack surface. This is especially evident when analyzing cyber risk to many of our Nation's supply chains. Critical infrastructure assets can be small businesses themselves or may be dependent on small businesses to provide essential services or materials. It is essential that small businesses implement common cybersecurity standards and practices to protect themselves and their customers. Small businesses face the same threats as large businesses, but do not necessarily have access to the same resources. DHS is working with our interagency partners to close this gap for cybersecurity information sharing, training, as well as resources.

As the Committee knows, DHS and the U.S. Small Business Administration have partnered to develop a strategy to help small- and medium-size businesses enhance their cybersecurity planning and risk management efforts. Small businesses are diverse in size and complexity, with varying needs for improving their cybersecurity posture. Because of this, it is imperative that we work with Small Business Development Centers across the country, as well as other information-sharing organizations. The federal government offers a suite of services and capabilities that can help small businesses improve their cybersecurity. For some, it may be simple training on cybersecurity beset practices or the implementation of basic cyber hygiene. For others, it may be performing complex vulnerability assessments to understand appropriate mitigation steps based on their specific risk profile. DHS offers a range of services to meet these needs and continues to pursue new opportunities to provide assistance.

In developing the small business cybersecurity strategy with the Small Business Administration, we have identified over 40 federal programs or initiatives that are helpful in assisting small businesses raise awareness of their cybersecurity posture. Some programs were created specifically for small businesses, while others provide assistance across a broader business community.

As our Nation continues to evolve and new threats emerge, we must not only develop more effective methods to protect our information systems, but also find more cost-effective and efficient ways to increase public awareness and access to cybersecurity resources. The Cybersecurity Act of 2015 established DHS as the federal government's central hub for the automated sharing of cyber threat indicators and defensive measures. Automated indicator sharing is part of the Department's efforts to create an ecosystem in which as soon as a company or federal agency observes malicious activity, the indicator associated with that activity can be shared in real-time at machine speed with all of our partners that are leveraging DHS's automated indicator-sharing service. This real-time sharing capability can limit the scalability of many attacks and thereby increasing the cost for the adversaries, as well as reducing the impact of malicious cyber activity. The automated indicator-sharing service is a relatively new capability, and we expect the volume of threat indicators shared through this system to substantially increase as technical standards, software, and hardware supporting the system continues to be refined and more businesses sign up. This approach to collective defense helps ensure that small- and medium-size businesses are protected using the best cyber defense available information.

Thank you for the opportunity to testify, and I look forward to your questions.

Chairman CHABOT. Thank you very much.

And I will now recognize myself to open the questions. And Mr. Driggers, I will start with you.

And I would like to begin with the Hikvision matter, and, first of all, it is my understanding that the Chinese government owned at least 40 percent of the company and maybe up to 42 is the figure we have been getting. Is that correct?

Mr. DRIGGERS. Yeah, that is what I have been seeing in reporting as well, sir.

Chairman CHABOT. Okay, thank you. And as I mentioned in my opening statement, there is a real concern regarding vulnerabilities in some of Hikvision's security cameras. I understand that the weakness made cameras remotely exploitable, and I also understand that when DHS became aware of the security exposure there was an advisory notice from DHS's cyber emergency response team and that Hikvision worked with DHS to fix the problem.

My question is this, is it likely that some small businesses could still be susceptible to this cybersecurity flaw? And how is DHS working to inform small businesses that they could be exposed to this risk?

Mr. DRIGGERS. So we publish our alerts on the US-CERT website, so that is open to the web, so anybody can access those. With access to this particular flaw, we did work with a research community. We discovered the vulnerability. We worked with the company and they put out a software update that mitigated the impacts of this particular exploitation. That is kind of standard practice that we do at the Department of Homeland Security across many different companies' devices and software, working to understand what vulnerabilities exist, and working with the companies to publish updates to their software so that we can close down and mitigate vulnerabilities. Certainly, if there are small businesses that are using devices and they are not patching those system or updating the software, they could be exposed to the vulnerability if they have not covered down on that particular update.

Chairman CHABOT. Okay, thank you.

Mr. Marshall, how do you determine whether a cyber attack on a small business warrants FBI intervention? Is there a monetary loss, threshold, or some other indicator to assess an appropriate level of response and/or dedication of resources from the FBI?

Mr. MARSHALL. There is no hard-and-fast rule, Mr. Chairman. Generally, there are a number of variables we will look at. It depends on the field office that has jurisdiction over the particular attack. It depends on the prosecutorial discretion of the U.S. Attorney's Office. Certainly, we are not going to dedicate resources to something that may not be prosecuted. The loss amount is certainly one of those things we would consider, and it is a variable in terms of say a \$100,000 loss in New York City may not draw our attention or resources, it may not get prosecuted, but a \$100,000 loss in Louisville, Kentucky, likely will. So there are a number of different factors.

We would also look at the attack vector, and if there was any interest, we still maintain our counterintelligence authorities and interest. We may look at it even though the loss amount is low and maybe it is not going to get prosecuted as a crime, but there are a number of different variables that would lead someone to make that determination.

Chairman CHABOT. Okay, thank you.

Mr. Driggers, let me go back to you. Does the Department of Homeland Security, or the FBI for that matter, leverage the Small Business Development Centers to assist small businesses in identifying and mitigating cybersecurity risks? And how effective has that partnership been if you do do that?

Mr. DRIGGERS. So we certainly work with many different information-sharing organizations, the Small Business Development Centers being one of those. Whether or not the Small Business Development Center itself has the technical acumen and the subject matter expertise to actually assist us with the particular support that we are providing a small business, that depends, but we certainly—I do not want to say 100 percent of the time we work through the Small Business Development Center, but if the small business is engaged with a Small Business Development Center and that is the way they want to engage the government, we would certainly go that route.

Chairman CHABOT. Okay. Thank you. And I have time for about one more question so I will go back to you, Mr. Marshall.

What steps are being taken by the FBI, and also by DHS, to guarantee that small businesses' personal information and IT data is protected? Are there any efforts to ensure that their information cannot be used against them in the future by some bad actors?

Mr. MARSHALL. Well, certainly, we would treat any information that we would come across through the course of investigation as evidence. And so it would absolutely get that protection from us. Our first and foremost responsibility when we respond to a scene is to pursue a criminal investigation. So we are not interested in collaborating necessarily with any regulatory agency. Certainly, we do not disseminate it to anyone else not directly involved in the investigation.

Chairman CHABOT. Okay. My time is expired, but let me just go real quick.

I assume DHS has policies in place to make sure that their personal information that they have is protected so it is not getting in the wrong hands. Is that correct, Mr. Driggers?

Mr. DRIGGERS. That is correct. We have a couple different information sharing handling caveats that we use, or handling processes that we use. We use a traffic light protocol, which is an international standard for safeguarding information. And we also use our liability coverage protections that we got with the Cybersecurity Information Sharing Act of 2015.

Chairman CHABOT. Okay. I thank both of you. My time is expired.

The Ranking Member is recognized for 5 minutes.

Ms. VELAZQUEZ. Thank you, Mr. Chairman.

I would like to address this question to both of you.

Based on your knowledge of and interaction with small firms, what is your opinion of the general state of small business cybersecurity? And is the federal government doing enough to help them and your agencies to improve it?

Mr. MARSHALL. I would tell you that they are underprepared. Even in the biggest firms, cybersecurity is oftentimes considered a cost center and the general thought process is that it is not necessarily the cost of doing business. So even in your bigger firms, cybersecurity is usually not something that is being considered. So as you go down the pecking order in terms of size when it comes to business ventures, when you get down to small businesses, I would tell you they are underprepared.

Ms. VELAZQUEZ. Thank you.

Yes, sir?

Mr. DRIGGERS. I would agree with Mr. Marshall. I would also say that each individual business needs to take a look at their risk profile. Not all businesses need the same cybersecurity posture. Cybersecurity mitigation and systems can be extremely costly so, you know, depending on what type of small business you are, the type of data you are holding, the services, whether you belong to a critical supply chain, you need to look at all of those factors in determining what types of security, cybersecurity mitigation steps you need to put in place.

Ms. VELAZQUEZ. Thank you.

Mr. Marshall, information sharing between the government and the private sector is critical to reducing national security breaches and cybercrime against Americans. Can you tell us how preventive information sharing is more effective for small firms from solely a cost perspective and how it assists the FBI in its role fighting cyber attacks?

Mr. MARSHALL. So to Mr. Driggers' point, not everybody has the same set of concerns. Not everybody is established or created a security posture that is forward leaning enough. So the hope is that the information we provide to them, whether it is indicators of compromise or a general awareness message about good cyber hygiene, the hope is that they can drill down and focus and spend whatever resources they are willing to commit to cybersecurity on those things. If we can provide them with IP addresses that they can block at their firewall, that is certainly more than what they would have had had we not provided information of that nature. We think it is absolutely critical to get the message out as far and wide as possible on the prevention side. Certainly, the fewer of these we have to investigate the better, obviously, but the more information we can provide the better. And we do tend to try to over communicate. Certainly, there are things that cannot be released because they are classified, either because of the way they were collected or what they are telling us about the adversary, but to the degree that we can declassify and push that information out we do, and we do it as quickly as possible.

Ms. VELAZQUEZ. So Mr. Driggers, we have 28 million small businesses in our country and knowledge is power. So if they are not aware of the threats in terms of cybersecurity attacks, they will not take any preventive measures. How can the federal government work in a way that raises awareness, especially for those small contractors that are doing business within the federal marketplace?

Mr. DRIGGERS. So I think that information sharing really underpins all the services and capabilities that we have at DHS with our cybersecurity programs. It is foundational to getting as much information out as we can, whether that is highly technical data and providing some context around that; or whether it is threat information or things like that, getting stuff declassified as much as we possibly can; or whether that is sharing machine-to-machine or just putting stuff out on our website or working with the FBI or these other information-sharing organizations, such as the ISACs or the ISAOs, Small Business Development Centers.

We also, obviously, work very closely under the National Infrastructure Protection Partnership model with the Sector Coordinating Councils. And so I think it is important to raise the awareness. We certainly need to do that. We need to use all available resources to do that and to get the information out as much as we possibly can.

Those organizations or those small businesses that are part of the supply chain, we are certainly sharing information with those individuals. Awareness is an issue. One of the objectives that you will see when we publish the small business strategy is a consolidation of resources and dedicated resources to do this outreach to the small business community to make sure that they understand what programs are available to assist them with their cybersecurity posture.

Ms. VELAZQUEZ. Thank you, Mr. Chairman.

Chairman CHABOT. The gentlelady's time is expired.

The gentleman from Kentucky, Mr. Comer, is recognized for 5 minutes.

Mr. COMER. Thank you, Mr. Chairman.

My first question for either witness, can you all walk me through your agency's protocol for responding to cyber threat indicators or reports of a cyber attack from a small business? In other words, what information do you need and how do you get the information?

Mr. MARSHALL. Sure. So we would get the information to our field offices one of two ways. Hopefully, there is an ongoing established relationship with the victim, either they are a member of InfoGard or some other group that has allowed us to create that relationship. If not, they tend to go through IC3 and report it there and then it is pushed to the appropriate field office. We would then have probably the cyber program coordinator in that field office make an assessment of what was written and then make contact, depending, again, depending upon the size of the breach, what was reported initially. If it is big enough, there would be probably coordination at the federal level here in Washington, D.C., but with field offices in 56 different locations, that would generically be how it would come to us. Then we would make an assessment probably through a phone call with the victim or somebody representing the victim whether or not to send resources and actually start opening investigation and start that process.

Mr. COMER. Many small businesses do not have preventive procedures in place to thwart a cyber attack before it happens. What do you suggest small businesses do to safeguard themselves against potential threats?

Mr. MARSHALL. Well, there are a number of things they can do, and I would suspect the best thing they could do is elevate the necessity for cybersecurity within their own organizations. Hire capable, competent people to help protect data. Create a culture within the organization that promotes security. It has got to be something you do every day. It cannot be done after the fact. So that would be my advice, is they need to be thinking about it on the front end.

Mr. DRIGGERS. I think there are some basic things that really all businesses can do. And some of these basic things individuals can do at home as well. You know, the bottom line is that an adversary is going to use the least cost tactic to get into a network, and so any time you can raise your security posture by doing simple basic things, they are going to bypass you and move on to the next target that may be more available so that they do not have to spend as many resources.

Certainly, backing up critical data is important for small businesses, particularly those that are holding a lot of sensitive, personal information about their customers' protecting their mobile devices, making sure that there is the ability to track, lock, as well as wipe any device that could be stolen or lost; protecting your organization against malware by making sure that you have a good patching schedule for software updates. A lot of companies that produce software and produce devices on a regular basis also produce security updates or software updates to those, and so it is important that you take advantage of that and you update your software, as well as protecting your data with passwords, two-factor authentication, changing default passwords on devices. These default passwords are available on the web, so it is important when you buy a new device that you change the default passwords on those. And I think some simple training for your employees about phishing attacks and the fact that those exist. That is a very low-tech, easy way for adversaries to get into networks. So doing that training for your employees is pretty low cost, and I think there is training available on the web for that.

Mr. COMER. Thank you, Mr. Chairman. I yield back.

Chairman CHABOT. The gentleman yields back.

The gentleman from South Carolina, Mr. Norman, is recognized for 5 minutes.

Mr. NORMAN. Thank you, Mr. Chairman.

I live in a rural district. A lot of small businesses. What would you say that the FBI, DHS could do to, I guess, avert the threat that they have? And secondly, to get people to talk about it. A lot of these firms will not talk about it because it is, for whatever reason, it is embarrassing. Either Mr. Driggers or Mr. Marshall, how would you respond to that?

Mr. DRIGGERS. Well, I think with regard to talking about it, I mean, that is an issue. Talking about it publicly could be an issue for a particular company. But what we want them to do is call the FBI or call the Department of Homeland Security, the National Cybersecurity and Communications Integration Center, so that we can take the steps necessary to help mitigate whatever incident happened, so that we can provide assistance to the impacted victim, and I think, even more importantly, learn what happened, develop analysis, and develop indicators so that we can share that more broadly so that other cyber network defenders can take advantage of the information. That said, when we do that we anonymize the information. We protect the identity of the victim through those information-sharing protocols that I talked about earlier.

Mr. MARSHALL. I would further that by saying maybe a better understanding of the fact that when you are a victim, we are going to continue to treat you as a victim. This is not a "gotcha game." This is not a, hey, we are going to run and tell a regulator or a State regulator that you were not properly prepared or defensed against these type of attacks. I understand the stigma to a degree because who wants to do business with someone that cannot protect their data? And you see that in small firms, and you see it in big firms, too. But what it will take to get over that stigma, I am not entirely sure.

We push the message repeatedly that, to Mr. Driggers' point, please call us. We certainly cannot do anything if we are not aware of it. But beyond that, pushing the message of better cybersecurity is probably all we can do.

Mr. NORMAN. What is your opinion? DHS oversees the National Cybersecurity and Communications Integration Center, which basically encourages the public and private sectors to swap information. Is this reliable? Is it worth the money? What is your take on that?

Mr. DRIGGERS. So it is absolutely reliable, and it has allowed us to, quite frankly, thwart many attacks to the analysis that we have done and the indicator sharing that we have pushed out either through our Automated Indicator Sharing System, which is, as I said in my opening statement, is a machine-to-machine, near real-time, as well as just publishing technical alerts with the technical information in there so that cyber network defenders can also take advantage of that, that are not necessarily leveraging that automated system. A lot of these technical alerts, the analysis is done at the National Cybersecurity and Communications Integration Center, but it is representative of whole government. So there is a lot of different interagency partners that are there to include the intelligence community as well as the FBI.

Mr. NORMAN. I yield back, Mr. Chairman.

Chairman CHABOT. The gentleman yields back.

The gentleman from Florida, Mr. Lawson, who is the Ranking Member of the Subcommittee on Health and Technology, is recognized for 5 minutes.

Mr. LAWSON. Thank you very much, Mr. Chairman. And welcome to the Committee.

And you all may already be aware of H.R. 4668 introduced by the chair here. Can you describe what challenges exist in the cybersecurity sphere as it relates to small business? How this bill may help to alleviate those challenges?

Mr. DRIGGERS. I certainly think the focus on small businesses and, quite frankly, I appreciate the Committee and the Chairman's focus on small businesses, particularly with regard to their cybersecurity. I think that putting more focus, making sure that we are attentive to the small business community and make sure that they are aware that there are resources that exist in the federal government that can help them and assist them with their cybersecurity activities and posture, that there are organizations like the 56 field offices that Mr. Marshall talked about, as well as the National Cybersecurity Communications Integration Center, that those organizations exist to provide assistance, to protect your information, to protect your identity. But the bottom line is we exist to support your efforts.

That said, we also want to work with the various different information-sharing organizations that are existing. The private sector has self-organized to create information-sharing and analysis centers, information-sharing and analysis organizations, the Small Business Development Centers. And we want to certainly work with them and through them to make sure that we are raising awareness about the various different programs that the federal government has to offer.

Mr. LAWSON. Okay. Mr. Marshall, do you want to comment?

Mr. MARSHALL. Anything that promotes cybersecurity would be beneficial. I referenced the NCFTA in my opening remarks. The original was opened in Pittsburgh, Pennsylvania, several years ago. It was wildly successful. It includes some smaller businesses, but we are expanding into New York. We are expanding into Los Angeles. And that model is one that we think is very effective.

Mr. LAWSON. Okay. When the question was asked earlier about small businesses in rural areas, how can these really small businesses—you know, I have a lot of rural areas back in my district. What incentives can you give to these "mom-and-pop" operations to really share cybersecurity data, and what do they get? What kind of cybersecurity will they inherit? You know, they are just a small-time operation.

Mr. MARSHALL. Hopefully, what they get, and we touched on this a little bit earlier, what they get are indicators of compromise and things that they can do quickly, cheaply, and effectively to try to stop some of the potential attacks against them. I do not know that they give up much more than their time to participate in things like InfraGard or even the business email compromise open houses or the ransomware open houses.

What they get is a better understanding of how the threat impacts them. A lot of these small businesses do not even know what business email compromise is. They probably do not know what phishing is. They probably do not know what ransomware is.

So just the hour that it would take to attend a meeting in an FBI field office or Secret Service field office to better understand the threat and get those things, as Mr. Driggers referred to, those things that will help them focus what they can invest on cybersecurity. They can really drill down and make sure that they are doing that very well. It will not stop everything, but to the point made earlier, if it makes you a less attractive target, then it is worth its investment in time.

Mr. LAWSON. The incentives to you, Mr. Driggers, that you might use is that they will grasp anything that they think is going to be harmful to their business operations, so how do you approach them?

Mr. DRIGGERS. Well, we approach them with the protections that we afford them, that we were given the authority for, to offer liability protection for information that they share with us. And I will tell you that just from a cultural perspective within DHS, particularly within the National Cybersecurity and Communications Integration Center that we call the NCCIC, protecting the identity of a victim underpins all the services and programs and the Information Sharing Protocols that we have. So you can rest assured, if you are going to share information with the NCCIC, that we are going to protect the identity of you. So there is a protection there, as well as a liability protection.

But to Mr. Marshall's point, just raising awareness, understanding that these types of threats are out there or these types of risk are out there, and doing some of the basic, very low-cost things that I kind of laid out before with regard to patching your networks, training your staff on email or on phishing attacks. You know, making sure that you have a simple policy in place that, you know, if there is a network email password that one employee has one password, that type of a thing, so you do not share passwords.

Mr. LAWSON. Okay. Thank you, Mr. Chairman. I yield back.

Chairman CHABOT. Thank you. The gentleman's time is expired.

The gentlelady from American Samoa, Mrs. Radewagen, who is the Chairman of the Subcommittee on Health and Technology, is recognized for 5 minutes.

Mrs. RADEWAGEN. Talofa and good morning. And I want to thank the Chairman for holding this hearing on this important issue.

As the Chairman of the Health and Technology Subcommittee, cybersecurity is something I care about deeply, and I want to thank you, Mr. Marshall and Mr. Driggers, for testifying before us today. Now, you gentlemen have already answered my first question, and I thank you for that.

My second issue is with foreign cyber threats, especially Chinese are out in our neck of the woods. The Chinese are making massive inroads with my neighbors in the South Pacific. And Mr. Marshall, what steps is the FBI taking to safeguard against sophisticated, state-backed cyber attackers? Furthermore, and this may be outside of the scope of this hearing, is there any technical assistance the United States may be able to provide for my neighbors who do not have the ability to counter these threats?

Mr. MARSHALL. I am not quite sure exactly which neighbors you are referring to. We get a tremendous amount of assistance from the NSA, from the agency. We certainly partner regularly with DHS. But we have a tremendous amount of technical assistance that helps us identify those threats and assess their intelligence value, and then come up with a comprehensive strategy to either mitigate them or monitor them.

Mrs. RADEWAGEN. My home district is American Samoa, as you may know, and so my neighbors are the Independent Nation of Samoa, Fiji, Tonga, and that part of the Pacific.

Mr. MARSHALL. We have a very good friend not that far away in Australia, and we do a lot of collaborative work with our Five Eye partners, of which they are one.

Mrs. RADEWAGEN. Thank you very much. I yield back the balance of my time, Mr. Chairman.

Chairman CHABOT. Thank you very much. The gentlelady yields back.

The gentleman from Iowa, Mr. Blum, who is Chairman of the Subcommittee on Agriculture, Energy, and Trade, is recognized for 5 minutes.

Mr. BLUM. Thank you, Chairman Chabot. And thank you to our panelists today for being here.

First question, kind of broad, I know, but how bad is this problem? I am a small businessman. I go back to my district and I talk to small business people every week and, you know, I can say, oh, you know, hey, cyber hacking, it is a big problem. It is a big deal. I do not think they really believe me. I mean, how bad is this problem? How can we quantify this? Is it getting better? Getting worse?

Mr. MARSHALL. Well, it is definitely getting worse.

Mr. BLUM. As evidenced by what?

Mr. MARSHALL. It is bad and getting worse. The number of cases that are referred for investigation. The number of attacks that are thwarted that we know that have been prevented. All of these numbers indicate a rise.

Mr. BLUM. A rise is a 2 percent rise? It has doubled? What kind of increase are we talking about?

Mr. MARSHALL. So if you wanted to narrow the question just a little bit further to look at something like business email compromise or ransomware, we are talking about in the neighborhood of 40 to 50 percent growth year over year. I do not have the exact numbers in front of me. Now, our hope is certainly that we can begin to do things as technology evolves and gives us other investigative opportunities that maybe we can figure out what the private sector had or maybe tamp some of these down. Indeed, I think that is happening.

Mr. BLUM. Is organized crime involved in this at all?

Mr. MARSHALL. Certainly, they are involved in it. I would say there are organized criminals around the world that have figured out how to branch into the cyberspace.

Mr. BLUM. I guess I do not mean organized criminals. I mean, organized crime, as in the Mafia and drug cartels and organizations like that?

Mr. MARSHALL. Yes. And you would be surprised at the areas in which they are looking. You mentioned drug cartels. If you were able to penetrate someone's air traffic system to determine or identify U.S. surveillance planes, would you be better or worse off? Things of that nature. Places where you would not normally expect to see.

Mr. BLUM. You bring that up. I fly 130 times a year, so I do care. I assume our air traffic control system is unbelievably secure. Not that it could not happen, but.

Mr. MARSHALL. It is, but it is not the only technology out there that helps monitor what is in the sky. And I use that just as an example. Can you monitor activity along the border—this may be a question better for you than for me—through introducing on somebody's network? Yes, you probably can. Would that be information that a drug cartel would be interested in? Sure, it would. So the answer to your question is yes.

Mr. BLUM. I assume some of these operations are relatively sophisticated?

Mr. MARSHALL. Yes.

Mr. BLUM. And maybe this would be a question for you, Mr. Driggers, Homeland Security. Are more of the cyber hackers domestic or are they foreign? And are they individuals or are they countries?

Mr. DRIGGERS. So I do not have the specific details as to whether they are foreign or domestic, or whether they are individuals or they are nation states. Certainly, we can make the assumption that all of those categories of adversary are working hard every day. They are certainly getting more sophisticated and they are getting more persistent, and we have seen that over the past at least 3 or 4 years.

But I also want to preference, particularly with the small business, it does not take sophistication to exploit a vulnerability in a small business. And I think all small businesses need to assume that they have some type of vulnerability that exists within their networks or the devices that they are using. And so it is really important that, because a lot of small businesses do not have the resources to really put in place very sophisticated cyber defense mechanisms, but they do have the resources to do the low-cost things that I talked about, and I think that that should be the focus and the awareness that we are talking about. We need to make sure that they are doing the basics with regard to cybersecurity hygiene, training their staff, and that they know who to call if there is a particular issue.

Mr. BLUM. I have often heard that warfare of the future will not be about bullets and bombs; it will be about bits and bytes. So this is a war. Are we winning the war or are we losing the war?

Mr. MARSHALL. As it pertains to the general public becoming more cybersecurity aware, I would say we are losing. Again, security is one of the last things people consider. Whether you are a small businessman or whether you are pulling a laptop out of its box for the first time when you set it up at home, these are just not things that we have been trained to think about. So in that regard I would say we are probably losing.

Mr. BLUM. Mr. Driggers, are we winning the war or are we losing the war?

Mr. DRIGGERS. So I will answer the same way Mr. Marshall did. I think if we look at the large businesses, particularly those that are designated as nationally critical infrastructure, and those from a risk profile that the Department of Homeland Security, you know, on a day-to-day basis interacts with, I think that they have certainly raised their game. But I think that there is a huge chasm between those individual businesses and the ones that are medium and small size.

Mr. BLUM. Thank you, gentlemen, and I yield back the time I do not have. Thank you.

Chairman CHABOT. Okay. The gentleman yields back.

And I just have one final question. When we have been discussing malware, just for those that may be watching at home or may see the transcript of this or whatever, we are essentially talking about your computer, your files, photographs, documents being seized by some criminal element or blackmailer or something that says I have got them now. I am not releasing this. I am not going to let you have access to your own computer unless you pay me X amount of money within a certain amount of time. And I guess that can happen to individuals on their home computer, or this is a Small Business Committee, so we are obviously most directly trying to help small businesses across the country. It can happen to anybody, but that is what we are talking about. Correct? I see you are both nodding.

If that should happen to a citizen or a small business, what should he or she do at that point? And either one of you or both of you, if you would like to.

Mr. MARSHALL. So the Bureau does not have an official position. What you are referring to is ransomware. The Bureau does not have an official position as to whether or not a victim of ransomware should, in fact, pay the ransom in order to get their data back. We have discussed a couple times that the important thing is to back up your data consistently so when this happens you can just ignore the request for ransom.

One of the things we would ask victims to consider is the fact that, one, they are being attacked by a criminal, so the promise of returning your data after payment should be considered by the person making the demand. The other thing is a lot of the malware variants now are locking data permanently. And you can pay a ransom, you can pay 100 times the ransom, there is no technical way to unlock our data.

So there is no formal advice. Different companies, big and small, have different types of responses to this, but we would ask that people consider the fact that a criminal is the one that is making the demand.

Chairman CHABOT. And I misspoke. I meant to say ransomware when I said malware, but it is a form of that.

Mr. Driggers, anything?

Mr. DRIGGERS. I would agree with Mr. Marshall. We do not necessarily have an official position. The individual business needs to make their own risk determination as to whether or not what action they take in terms of responses to some type of ransomware attack.

Chairman CHABOT. Thank you very much.

The gentleman from New York, Mr. Espaillat, is recognized for 5 minutes.

Mr. ESPAILLAT. Thank you, Chairman.

Mr. Marshall, the FBI's Cyber Division addresses a wide variety of issues, including nontraditional forms of cybercrimes. What is the most common form of cyber attack your division encounters? Is it different from small business complaints that you process on a regular basis? Are businesses coming forward as well?

Mr. MARSHALL. Sure. I would tell you the most frequent attack vector is spear phishing. It happens repeatedly, over and over and over again, and we have talked about the amount of money it costs to have good cybersecurity and cyber hygiene. The bottom line is if somebody can send out 10 million emails, it just takes one employee not paying attention to click on it to thwart your multi-million investment in cybersecurity. I will not go down the laundry list of breaches that we have had in the last year, but I think a lot of them have that component in common. And I do not have an exact number for you, but a vast majority of them are through a spear phish campaign.

Mr. ESPAILLAT. Okay. And Mr. Driggers, the Obama administration made efforts to increase cybersecurity by creating a federal privacy panel and creating sanctions to block those that pose a significant threat. How are these efforts beneficial to small businesses? And what more remains to be done in this particular area?

Mr. DRIGGERS. Well, Congressman, I do not have a lot of details on the panel. I can certainly take that back and get the information and respond to you.

Mr. ESPAILLAT. And finally, I will ask both of you. I have had several discussions with experts regarding cybersecurity in general, and they have told me that basically, if somebody wants to hack you, if they are really intent on doing this, there is basically very little we can do about it. They can penetrate eventually at some point or another. Is that the case? Are we at the mercy of these hackers? And is there anything we can do to prevent it? I mean, America should not be at the mercy of folks that may have an intent to do something and cannot be stopped. Is there anything that we can do to stop this?

Mr. MARSHALL. If the question is, is there a magic bullet or a silver bullet that will put an end to this, the answer is no. There are things that you can do, an escalating series of things you can do to try to avoid becoming a victim, everything from simple awareness and then a "Do not click this email" campaign, all the way up to the most sophisticated technical, advanced technical protections and defenses that include encryption and routine backups. It depends upon what kind of money you are willing to spend, but I do not believe that there is a magic bullet that will just make this problem go away.

Mr. ESPAILLAT. Thank you, Mr. Chairman. I yield my time.

Chairman CHABOT. Thank you. The gentleman yields back.

As the hearing comes to a close, we want to again thank our witnesses here this morning for, and now right after this afternoon as well, for being here and going over one of the topics that this Committee considers to be one of the chief challenges that small businesses face across the country. And we appreciate the information that you have given us.

We also appreciate, the chair appreciates working with the Ranking Member on legislation, H.R. 4668 as it moves forward.

I would ask unanimous consent that members have 5 legislative days to submit statements and supporting materials for the record.

Without objection, so ordered.

And if there is no further business to come before the Committee, we are adjourned. Thank you very much.

[Whereupon, at 12:04 p.m., the Committee was adjourned.]

APPENDIX

Department of Justice

STATEMENT OF
HOWARD S. MARSHALL
DEPUTY ASSISTANT DIRECTOR
CYBER DIVISION
FEDERAL BUREAU OF INVESTIGATION

BEFORE THE
HOUSE COMMITTEE ON SMALL BUSINESS
UNITED STATES HOUSE OF REPRESENTATIVES

AT A HEARING ENTITLED
"SMALL BUSINESS INFORMATION SHARING:
COMBATING FOREIGN CYBER THREATS"

PRESENTED
JANUARY 30, 2018

**STATEMENT OF
HOWARD S. MARSHALL
DEPUTY ASSISTANT DIRECTOR
CYBER DIVISION
FEDERAL BUREAU OF INVESTIGATION**

**BEFORE THE
HOUSE COMMITTEE ON SMALL BUSINESS
UNITED STATES HOUSE OF REPRESENTATIVES**

**AT A HEARING ENTITLED
"SMALL BUSINESS INFORMATION SHARING: COMBATING FOREIGN CYBER THREATS"**

**PRESENTED
JANUARY 30, 2018**

Chairman Chabot, Ranking Member Velázquez, and members of the committee, thank you for the invitation to provide remarks on the FBI's role in helping small businesses defend against cyber threats. We consider engagement with the private sector to be a significant factor in our mission to identify, pursue, and defeat nefarious cyber criminals and enemies of the United States.

As the committee is well aware, the growing number and sophistication of cyber threats poses a critical risk to U.S. businesses, and the impact of a successful attack can be devastating to small businesses in particular. We continue to see an increase in the scale and scope of reporting on malicious cyber activity that can be measured by the amount of corporate data stolen or deleted, personally identifiable information compromised, or remediation costs incurred by U.S. victims. Some of the more prevalent or rising cyber threats to small businesses include the following.

Business E-mail Compromise

Business E-mail Compromise ("BEC") is a scam targeting businesses working with foreign suppliers or businesses that regularly perform wire transfer payments. By compromising legitimate business e-mail accounts through social engineering or computer intrusion techniques, criminals are able to conduct unauthorized transfers of funds. Notably, BEC scams have been reported in all 50 States and have resulted in hundreds of millions of dollars in losses to U.S. businesses and individuals.

The victims of BEC scams range from small businesses to large corporations across a variety of services. The BEC threat is highly adaptable and constantly evolving, but criminals have been particularly active in targeting small to large companies and individuals which may transfer high-dollar funds or sensitive records in the course of business. BEC compromises can be facilitated through a variety of vectors, including social engineering, phishing scams that lure victims to click on malware brute force cracking of e-mail passwords, or the obtaining of e-mail credentials online. An actor will use one or more of these vectors to steal the victim's credentials, impersonate a person with authority to request payments or records, and obtain access to data and e-mail for the purposes of theft; or to impersonate a legitimate vendor or business contact to trick the victim into paying an invoice or transferring payroll records to the actor's account.

The sophistication of BEC actors varies. In general, transnational organized crime groups may invest more time and resources in high-dollar targets. On the other hand, less sophisticated actors, who likely account for the majority of attempts, steal smaller sums using spoofed e-mails sent in bulk or through e-mail contact with a presumably vulnerable target. Unfortunately, both types of actors can be successful if victims are not vigilant. Popular BEC targets include third-party payroll companies, parties involved in real estate transactions (including buyers, sellers, realtors, and title companies), firms offering legal services, and import and export companies.

When we engage with the private sector, we encourage companies to take certain precautions to safeguard their systems, records, and data. We recommend that businesses require a secondary, independent verification of any payment requests or changes to existing beneficiary accounts; that they use complicated passwords or long passphrases for company and personal e-mail accounts, change passwords regularly, and not use the same password for multiple accounts; implement two-factor authentication; and that they utilize commercial antivirus and anti-spyware products. We also recommend they avoid doing formal business on free web-based e-mail accounts; establish a company domain name and limit formal communications to company e-mail accounts; and, if possible, create intrusion detection system filters that flag e-mails with extensions that are similar to company e-mail.

Ransomware

Ransomware is a type of malware used to encrypt an individual's or organization's files and documents, making them unreadable until a ransom is paid. Ransomware targets both human and technical weaknesses in organizations and individual networks to deny the availability of critical data or systems. Ransomware is a simple and proven model that continues to yield profits for cyber criminals. The attacks are difficult to attribute, and they do not require "money mule" networks (i.e., people involved in transferring illegally obtained money on behalf of someone else) to cash out. Malicious cyber actors are increasingly using virtual currency, such as bitcoin, to facilitate their crimes. Mixers, tumblers, and other anonymizing services create challenges for tracing and attribution. While these services use different mechanisms and approaches, they obfuscate the source and destination of funds by mixing funding streams, adding extra layers, or combining transactions.

In short, ransomware actors are using more sophisticated tools that allow the malware to propagate faster, and the campaigns are becoming bigger and causing more damage. For these reasons, we can expect ransomware to remain a significant threat to businesses in the U.S. and worldwide. Popular targets include hospitals, law firms, and businesses needing immediate access to their data. Two typical infection methods include clicking on malicious phishing e-mail links and visiting infected websites. Remote Desktop Protocol, a program that allows one computer to remotely operate another, can also be used as a vector.

Once a machine is infected, typically all files on local and attached drives are encrypted and effectively locked away from the user. The criminal notifies the victim they must pay a ransom in order to receive a digital key to unlock and retrieve their files. It is important to note that even if a ransom is paid, there is no guarantee the business or individual will obtain their files from the cyber criminal.

To guard against the ransomware threat, we encourage businesses to schedule regular data backups to drives not connected to their network. These drives can be used to restore a system to the backup version without paying the ransom to the perpetrator. Additional guidance from the FBI for guarding against ransomware is available at https://www.fbi.gov/file-repository/ransomware-prevention-and-response-for-cisos.pdf/view.

Criminal Data Breach Activity

Cyber criminals are continuously looking for vulnerabilities in the networks of U.S. businesses of all sizes, as well as prominent public and private sector officials. Cyber criminals are looking for entry into any network that contains personal or financial information of employees or customers that can be monetized or posted online. Some actors also seek to encrypt corporate data so it can be ransomed. Vectors can range from the use of phishing e-mails in order to steal login credentials to crafting malware to exploit sensitive, vulnerable systems.

Business networks often contain financial information such as credit card and bank account information, as well as personally identifiable information such as names and social security numbers. Consequently, we encourage businesses to apply a variety of best practices to secure their network architecture, network activity, and user data as much as possible in order to make it more difficult for an adversary to compromise their infrastructure.

Internet of Things

Internet of Things ("IoT") devices and embedded systems are becoming widespread in business, government, and home networks. They provide low-cost, real-time monitoring and automation services to users. The information these devices collect provides billions of data sets useful in analyzing productivity, marketing, consumer and market trends, and user behavior and demographics. However, IoT devices could be compromised by cyber actors taking advantage of lax security standards and inherent device connectivity to increase the impact of cyber attacks, or as a pivot point into personal or corporate networks. Increased connectivity through IoT devices will only increase the potential attack surface for networks, as cybersecurity is largely under-prioritized from device design through implementation.

In September 2016, an IoT botnet was used to conduct one of the largest Distributed-Denial-of-Service ("DDoS") attacks ever recorded. Similar attacks have since taken place. These attacks have resulted in widespread Internet outages and are very costly to victims. The source code for multiple IoT malware variants are publicly available, making it easy for cyber actors to create their own IoT botnet. Since October 2017, new IoT malware variants are targeting and exploiting firmware vulnerabilities, increasing the number of devices vulnerable to compromise. Individuals and businesses can prevent their devices from being compromised by changing default user name and passwords, ensuring device firmware is up to date, implementing strong firewall rules, and by turning off or rebooting devices when not in use. The FBI has issued guidance on securing IoT devices through Public Service Announcements, published on the Internet Crime Complaint Center's ("IC3") website at www.ic3.gov. In addition, guidance from the Department of Justice for securing IoT devices is available at https://www.justice.gov/criminal-ccips/page/file/984001/download. Other agencies are working to address this challenge as well, notably, the Department of Commerce's National Institute of Standards and Technology, which is in the process of collaborating with businesses, academia, and government stakeholders to develop standards, guidelines, and related tools to improve the cybersecurity of IoT devices.

FBI Cyber Private Sector Engagement

In light of these and other cyber threats to U.S. businesses, the FBI has made private sector engagement a key component of our strategy for combatting cyber threats. Recognizing the ever-changing landscape of cyber threats, the FBI is enhancing the way it communicates with private industry. Traditionally, the FBI used information developed through its investigations, shared by intelligence community partners, or provided by other law enforcement agencies to understand the threat posed by nation states and criminal actors. However, we are now also looking to integrate private industry information into our intelligence cycle to enhance our ability to identify and respond to both emerging and ongoing threats. We also utilize our intelligence to prioritize sector engagement and potential vulnerabilities. Private industry has unique insight into their own networks and may have information as to why their company, or their sector, may be an attractive target for malicious cyber activity. Companies may also be able to share intelligence on the types of attempted attacks they experience. We believe it is important the FBI integrate this type of data into its own intelligence cycle. As we move forward to enhance our sector-specific analysis capabilities, we are looking to private industry to help us gain a better understanding of their companies and their respective sectors. This type of information sharing enables us to provide more specific, actionable, and timely information to our industry partners so they can protect their systems in a proactive manner.

In fiscal year 2017, FBI Cyber Division reorganized its analytic and outreach resources to focus on this intelligence-driven approach to FBI engagement with critical infrastructure entities on cyber threats. FBI Cyber Division has published Intelligence Directed Queries that direct field offices to address collection needs in cyber space when engaging with sector partners.

In addition, the FBI disseminates information regarding specific threats to the private sector through various reporting mechanisms. Public Service Announcements ("PSAs"), published by the Internet Crime Complaint Center ("IC3") on www.ic3.gov, provide timely and practical information to U.S. businesses and individuals on the latest threats and scams. Each PSA typically contains information about a threat, warnings signs and indicators businesses should look for, precautions organizations should take to protect their data and networks, and steps for mitigation in the event of a compromise. We have released nearly 70 of these announcements over the past five years, including seven in 2017 that addressed such topics as Business E-mail Compromise, IoT vulnerabilities, and tactics being used by nefarious actors to launch DDoS attacks.

We also offer several other types of reports to the private sector, including Private Industry Notifications ("PINs"), which provide contextual information about ongoing or emerging cyber threats, and FBI Liaison Alert System ("FLASH") reports, which provide technical indicators gleaned through investigations or intelligence. These communication methods facilitate the sharing of information with a broad audience or specific sector and are intended to provide recipients with actionable intelligence to aid in victim notifications, threat neutralization, and other investigative efforts. In some instances, the FBI may work with other government agencies to release joint products for private industry. These joint products my include Joint Intelligence or Indicator Bulletins ("JIB"), Joint Analysis Reports ("JAR"), or other miscellaneous products.

The FBI believes it is critical to maintain strong relationships with private sector organizations to allow for the successful responses to cyber attacks. One example of an effective public/private relationship is the National Cyber-Forensics and Training Alliance ("NCFTA"), a nonprofit 501(3)(c) corporation focused on identifying, mitigating, and neutralizing cybercrime threats globally. Working hand in hand with private industry, law enforcement, and academia, the NCFTA's mission is to provide a neutral, trusted environment that enables two-way information sharing, collaboration, and training. The NCFTA works directly with 136 member organizations from the banking, retail, critical infrastructure, healthcare, and government sectors. NCFTA recently expanded from its headquarters location in Pittsburgh and is now operating additional offices in New York City and Los Angeles.

The FBI Cyber Division regularly coordinates initiatives for engagement with private sector partners to prevent threats and ultimately close intelligence gaps. In recent years, we have launched public awareness campaigns or "open houses" to educate businesses on serious cyber threats. In 2016, the FBI collaborated with the Department of Homeland Security ("DHS"), U.S. Secret Service ("USSS"), Department of Health and Human Services ("HHS"), and the National Council of Information Sharing and Analysis Centers ("NC-ISACs") to host conferences and workshops at FBI and USSS field offices across the country to educate businesses on the ransomware threat. The FBI and USSS jointly hosted these workshops in 14 key cities, targeting small, medium, and large organizations. Over 5,700 individuals were briefed during this campaign.

Similarly, in 2017, the FBI collaborated with DHS, USSS, and NC-ISAC to host workshops on the BEC threat in strategically identified locations across the country. These workshops were launched in October of 2017 to coincide with National Cyber Security Awareness Month and continued into early fiscal year 2018. Nearly 2,500 business leaders were briefed during this campaign.

The FBI Cyber Division continues to engage directly with businesses in other ways as well. The FBI Cyber Division either hosts or participates in briefings, conferences, workshops, and other meetings providing strategic-level information to key executives throughout industry. These briefings include both classified and unclassified discussions regarding cyber threats. Over the past five years, the FBI Cyber Division has completed nearly 2,800 such engagements, not counting the many informal contacts and interactions we have with businesses on a regular basis.

In addition, the FBI leverages its unique, decentralized field office model to ensure it can engage effectively with small and local businesses across the country and work side-by-side with State and local law enforcement for the furtherance of cyber investigations. The FBI is made up of 56 field offices spanning all 50 States and U.S. territories, each with a multi-agency Cyber Task Force ("CTF") modeled after the successful Joint Terrorism Task Force program. The task forces bring together cyber investigators, prosecutors, intelligence analysts, computer scientists, and digital forensic technicians from various Federal, State, and local agencies present within the office's territory. Our field-centric business model allows us to develop relationships with local businesses, companies and organizations, putting us in an ideal position to engage with potential victims of cyber attacks and crimes. Cyber-trained special agents are in each field office, providing locally available expertise to deploy to victim sites immediately upon notice of an incident. Computer scientists and intelligence analysts are also stationed in field offices to support incident response efforts and provide intelligence collection and analysis as well as technical assistance and capability.

The Bureau has had success with operating joint investigations with local law enforcement through our Cyber TFOs to dismantle large criminal enterprises engaging in computer intrusion and cyber-enabled crimes. Additionally, the Bureau works with local law enforcement on various Internet fraud matters through our Operation Wellspring platform, through which we package complaints from the Internet Crime Complaint Center ("IC3") and provide them to local law enforcement to work independently or in coordination with their local FBI field office.

Recognizing small businesses often engage State and local law enforcement as a first line of defense during a cyber incident, the Bureau offers our State and local partners access to FBI cyber training, including private sector training that offers certifications in the cyber security industry. The FBI's Cyber Division—working with the International Association of Chiefs of Police ("IACP") and cyber experts from Carnegie Mellon University—has developed the Cyber Investigator Certification Program ("CICP"). This self-guided, online training program is available free of charge to all local, State, Tribal, territorial, and Federal law enforcement personnel and provides training in how to conduct effective cyber investigations.

When a small business has been victimized by a cybercrime and reaches out to the FBI for assistance, we coordinate with the individual business to determine the best course of action to address the incident. The FBI's approach in working with potential or actual victims of cyber intrusions or attacks is to first and foremost, and to the best of our ability, use our processes to protect the victim from being re-victimized, and to provide confidentiality and discretion during the investigative process. No matter what course of action is deemed appropriate, the FBI views a company that has been attacked as a victim and will protect investigative information appropriately. Our goal in each instance to work with the business side by side to investigate the systems and data at play in the incident. We will work with the victim to determine attribution, which can lead to prosecution of the subject. Through its work with other government agencies, the FBI and Department of Justice can provide information that can be used to initiate indictments, affect arrests, generate demarches, or produce international sanctions against those who conduct cyber attacks or aggressive actions against entities in the United States.

We at the FBI appreciate this committee's efforts in making cyber threats to small businesses a focus and to committing to improving how we can work together to better defend U.S. business from cyber adversaries. We thank you for the opportunity to speak about our cyber outreach efforts; we look forward to discussing these issues in greater detail and answering any questions you may have.

Statement for the Record

Of

Richard Driggers
Deputy Assistant Secretary for Cybersecurity and Communications
National Protection and Programs Directorate
U.S. Department of Homeland Security

Before the United States House of Representatives
Committee on Small Business

Regarding

Foreign Cybersecurity Threats to America's Small Businesses

January 30, 2018

Chairman Chabot, Ranking Member Velázquez, and members of the Committee, thank you for the opportunity to be here today. Safeguarding and securing cyberspace is a core mission at the Department of Homeland Security (DHS). I am pleased to be here today discussing our efforts to reduce and mitigate cybersecurity risk to the Nation's small businesses.

The National Protection and Programs Directorate (NPPD) is responsible for protecting civilian Federal Government networks; sharing information related to cybersecurity risks and incidents and providing technical assistance to federal agencies, as well as state, local, tribal, and territorial (SLTT) governments, international partners and the private sector; and coordinating certain aspects of the Federal Government's incident response activities to defend against cyber threats. We endeavor to enhance cyber threat information-sharing across the globe to stop cyber incidents before they start and help businesses and government agencies to protect their networks and quickly recover should such a cyber incident occur. By bringing together all levels of government, the private sector, international partners, and the public, we are taking action to protect against cybersecurity risks, improve our whole-of-government incident response capabilities, enhance information sharing on best practices and cyber threats, and to strengthen resilience.

There are over 30 million small businesses in the U.S. employing over 47 percent of the Nation's population and comprising over 97 percent of total businesses in North America. As small businesses become increasingly reliant on information technology, so do the cybersecurity risks they face. Malicious cyber activity can severely harm small business operations and reduce consumer confidence. The Department of Homeland Security, Department of Justice, Small Business Administration, and other interagency partners play a crucial role in helping small businesses identify and mitigate these risks.

Threats

Cyber threats remain one of the most significant strategic risks for the United States, threatening our national security, economic prosperity, and public health and safety. The past year has marked a turning point in the cyber domain. We have long been confronted with a myriad of malicious cyber activities against our digital networks. But over the past year, Americans saw advanced persistent threat actors, including hackers, cyber criminals, and nation states, increase the frequency and sophistication of malicious cyber activity. Our adversaries have been developing and using advanced cyber capabilities to undermine critical infrastructure, target our livelihoods and innovation, steal our national security secrets, and threaten our democracy through attempts to manipulate elections.

Global cyber incidents, such as the "WannaCry" ransomware incident in May of last year and the "NotPetya" malware incident in June, are examples of malicious actors leveraging cyberspace to create disruptive effects and cause economic loss. Incidents like these are indiscriminate, and the Nation's small businesses are often victims. These incidents exploited known vulnerabilities in software commonly used across the globe. Prior to these events, NPPD had already taken actions to help protect networks from similar malicious cyber activities.

Through requested vulnerability scanning, NPPD helped stakeholders identify vulnerabilities on their networks so they could be patched before these cyber incidents occurred. Recognizing that not all users are able to install patches immediately, NPPD shared additional mitigation guidance to assist network defenders. As the incidents unfolded, NPPD led the Federal Government's incident response efforts, working with our interagency partners, including providing situational awareness, information sharing, malware analysis, and technical assistance to affected entities.

Supporting the Nation's Small Businesses against Cyber Risks

Small businesses play a key role in ensuring the security, reliability, and resilience of the Nation's critical infrastructure. The Homeland Security Act authorizes NPPD's National Cybersecurity and Communications Integration Center (NCCIC) to assist small businesses through the dissemination of information on cyber threat indicators, defensive measures, cybersecurity risks, incidents, analyses, and warnings. Critical infrastructure owners and operators depend on small businesses to provide equipment and services and small businesses rely on having a reputation of a trusted business partner. It is essential that small businesses adopt common cybersecurity standards and practices to protect themselves and their customers. Small businesses face the same threats as large business, but do not necessarily have access to the same resources or information as large businesses. NPPD is working with our interagency partners to close the gap for cybersecurity information sharing, training, and resources.

The Federal Government and its contractors, subcontractors, and suppliers at all tiers of the supply chain are under constant attack, targeted by increasingly sophisticated and well-funded adversaries seeking to steal, compromise, alter or destroy sensitive information. In some cases, advanced threat actors target small businesses deep in the government's supply chain to gain a foothold and then pivot to sensitive information and intellectual property. Over the last several years, many federal contractors have significantly improved their cybersecurity posture, making it more difficult for threat actors to launch successful attacks on their enterprises. However, this has caused increased targeting of small businesses connected to the federal supply chain that may not have the resources or awareness to adequately address such threats.

DHS and the U.S. Small Business Administration have partnered to develop a strategy pursuant to the requirements in section 1841 of the National Defense Authorization Act for Fiscal Year 2017 (Pub. L. No. 114-328) to help small and medium-sized businesses enhance their cybersecurity planning and risk management efforts.

In order to develop a strategy that effectively responds to stakeholders' needs, the America's Small Business Development Centers (ASBDC) conducted a nationwide survey soliciting feedback on the cybersecurity needs of small businesses. Over 85 percent of small business owners fear cyber incidents and feel unprepared to handle one. Despite the expressed need for resources to address cyber concerns, 70 percent of respondents said they were not aware of available resources and only 7.7 percent indicated they looked for resources from Federal Government sources. More than half of respondents indicated they need skills in small business defensive and response strategies.

These responses demonstrate the need to take a different approach engaging small businesses compared to large corporations or other federal agencies. Small businesses are diverse in size and complexity, with varying needs for improving their cybersecurity posture. For some, it may be basic training related to cyber hygiene and for others, it may be complex vulnerability assessments. To effectively address the cybersecurity needs of small businesses, the Federal Government must be able to identify the most relevant resources and information and provide those resources and information in an efficient and cost-effective fashion. This involves not only a centralized location with access to all existing federal cybersecurity information and resources, but also a way to match the appropriate resources to the specific needs of small businesses.

Fortunately, the Department of Homeland Security already offers or supports an array of cybersecurity programs, projects, and activities that are applicable to small businesses. In developing the small business development center cyber strategy, we identified at least 46 federal programs or initiatives that small businesses can utilize. Some programs were created specifically for small businesses, while others serve a larger critical infrastructure audience. Increasing awareness and access to these resources, which are available at little to no cost, can increase the cybersecurity of small businesses.

Furthermore, NPPD promotes cybersecurity tools, best practices, and services to the small business community. This is a focal point for cybersecurity outreach, education, and information for the Nation's 16 critical infrastructure sectors as well as small and medium-sized businesses. NPPD cybersecurity resources include technical assistance; voluntary assessments; sector-specific implementation guidance; cybersecurity publications for business and government agencies; cybersecurity awareness raising materials; a suite of services for conducting risk assessments and enhancing information sharing; and cyber workforce development and training programs. NPPD continues to work on expanding awareness of these resources among small businesses.

Information sharing and safeguarding information is a key pillar of effective cybersecurity. By appropriately sharing information while protecting personally identifiable information rapidly between government and the private sector, network defenders can block cyber threats or limit the effects of compromised systems. Last year, the President signed Executive Order (EO) 13800, on *Strengthening the Cybersecurity of Federal Networks and Critical Infrastructure*. This EO set in motion a series of assessments and deliverables to understand how to improve our defenses and lower our risk to cyber threats. DHS has led collaborative efforts with federal and private sector partners to accomplish the range of actions included in the EO. Many of the initiatives NPPD has developed and improved upon can be applied to small businesses.

The NPPD's NCCCI serves as the hub of information sharing activities for DHS to increase awareness of vulnerabilities, incidents, and mitigation. Within the NCCIC, the Cyber Information Sharing and Collaboration Program (CISCP) is NPPD's flagship program for public-private information sharing and complements other DHS information sharing efforts. In CISCP, DHS and participating companies share information about cyber threats, incidents, and vulnerabilities. CISCP is free of charge and available to any company with an interest in multi-directional cybersecurity information sharing and robust collaboration.

By sharing information quickly and widely, we help all partners block cyber threats before damaging incidents occur. Equally important, the information we receive from partners helps us identify emerging risks and develop effective protective measures.

Moreover, as required by the Cybersecurity Act of 2015, we established a capability, known as Automated Indicator Sharing (AIS), to automate our sharing of cyber threat indicators in real time. AIS is a part of the Department's effort to create an environment where as soon as a company or federal agency observes an attempted compromise, the indicator is shared at machine speed with all of our partners, enabling them to protect themselves from that particular threat. This real-time sharing capability can limit the scalability of malicious cyber activities, thereby increasing the costs for adversaries and reducing the impact of malicious cyber activity. An ecosystem built around automated sharing and network defense-in-depth should enable organizations to detect and thwart the most common malicious cyber activity, freeing their cybersecurity staff to concentrate on the novel and sophisticated malicious cyber activity.

More than 230 agencies and private sector partners have connected to the AIS capability. Notably, partner organizations include partners, information sharing and analysis organizations (ISAOs) and computer emergency response teams, which further share with or protect their customers and stakeholders, significantly expanding the impact of this capability and accessibility to smaller businesses. The AIS technologies and policy are structured in a way that protects the identity of our partners, and the information shared is limited to cyber threat information, which protects privacy and civil liberties. AIS is still a new capability and we expect the volume of threat indicators shared through this system to substantially increase as the technical standards, software, and hardware supporting the system continue to be refined and put into full production. As more indictors are shared from other federal agencies, SLTT governments, and the private sector, this information sharing environment will become more robust and effective. This approach to collective defense helps ensure that small and medium-sized businesses are protected using the best defense information available, including information from larger and more sophisticated companies and our own government sources.

Supply Chain Risk Management

Supply chain risk is another area that has gained increasing prominence and concern in recent years. When the Federal Government—or its contractors at any tier of the supply chain—acquire a solution that has inadequate cybersecurity built in, the government ultimately incurs increased risk throughout the lifespan and disposal of that product or service. This remain the case until the government incurs the often more expensive cost of fixing the vulnerability after its incorporation. The lasting effect of inadequate built in cybersecurity in acquired items is part of what makes supply chain risk management so important to achieving cybersecurity and resiliency.

Offshore sourcing by information and communications technology (ICT) manufacturers and sellers has demonstrated its merit as a means to reduce costs. And as a result, most ICT is now produced in a global supply chain. Movement of production outside the U.S. has led to growing concerns associated with foreign ownership, control, manipulation, or influence over items that are purchased by the government and used in or connected to critical infrastructure or mission essential systems.

To appropriately address supply chain risks, it is critical to understand that the problem is not a simple function of geography. While there are certainly countries that provide environments that are more conducive to nefarious supply chain activities, pedigree is only a sub-set of factors to consider in supply chain risk assessments. There are more important factors to address the security or integrity of components and end items, including careful attention to the people, processes, and technology used to develop, deliver, operate, and dispose of the products and services used by the government and its contractors. Additionally, it is important to note that most known incidents are not caused by an adversary intentionally inserting malicious code into an ICT component through its supply chain, but are made through exploitation of unintentional vulnerabilities in code or components due to inadequate security practices in the manufacturing and integration processes.

Last year, the President signed EO 13806 on *Assessing and Strengthening the Manufacturing and Defense Industrial Base and Supply Chain Resiliency of the United States.* The Department of Homeland Security has worked with the Department of Defense to identify key supply chain risks. In parallel to this, NPPD has established a Cyber Supply Chain Risk Management (C-SCRM) Initiative under the Office of Cybersecurity and Communications to address risks to our ICT supply chains. The objective of the C-SCRM initiative is to enable stakeholders to be smarter consumers of ICT products and services by providing timely, robust, actionable information about supply chain risks and mitigations to users, buyers, manufacturers, and sellers of ICT.

While the ICT supply chain is not the source of all cyber risk, it presents opportunity for creation of threats and vulnerabilities, and ICT enables the connectivity that is a necessary element for cyber exploitation. Commercial ICT is ubiquitous in federal networks, even those that handle the most sensitive information and support essential functions of the government. Therefore, the C-SCRM Initiative will focus primarily on exposure to cyber risks related to acquisitions of ICT and how those risks should be addressed. However, due to the increasing connectivity of the world and the growing sophistication of threats, the initiative will also address acquisitions that are outside the boundaries of traditional definitions of ICT, including connected Internet of Things devices such as automobiles and industrial control systems. In 2018, the C-SCRM initiative will begin identifying and mitigating supply chain threats and vulnerabilities to Federal High Value Assets. In the following year, the C-SCRM Initiative will expand in scope to conduct due diligence on proposed contractors and subcontractors for individual acquisitions, provide public-private stakeholders unclassified supply chain risk information, and establish trusted supplier and product lists.

Conclusion

In the face of increasingly sophisticated threats, NPPD stands on the front lines of the Federal Government's efforts to defend our Nation's critical infrastructure from natural disasters, terrorism and adversarial threats, and technological risk such as those caused by cyber threats. Our infrastructure environment today is complex and dynamic with interdependencies that add to the challenge of securing and making it more resilient. Small businesses play an important role in protecting and securing our Nation's critical infrastructure as they are important players in effective supply risk management. The Federal Government possesses a suite of programs and capabilities that can improve cybersecurity for small businesses. However, not all small businesses require the same type of resources. DHS is able offer a range of services to meet these needs and continues to pursue new opportunities to provide assistance. As our Nation continues to evolve and new threats emerge, we must not only develop more effective methods to safeguard our information systems, but also find more cost-effective and efficient ways to increase public awareness and access to cybersecurity resources.

Thank you for the opportunity to testify, and I look forward to any questions you may have.